D0926736

Energy for Today

# Wind Power

By Tea Benduhn

Reading consultant: Susan Nations, M.Ed.,
author/literacy coach/consultant in literacy development

Science and curriculum consultant: Debra Voege, M.A.,
science curriculum resource teacher

WEEKLY READER®
PUBLISHING

**Please visit our web site at www.garethstevens.com.**
**For a free color catalog describing our list of high-quality books,**
**call 1-800-542-2595 (USA) or 1-800-387-3178 (Canada). Our fax: 1-877-542-2596**

**Library of Congress Cataloging-in-Publication Data**

Benduhn, Tea.
Wind power / by Tea Benduhn.
p. cm. — (Energy for today)
Includes bibliographical references and index.
ISBN-10: 0-8368-9265-8 — ISBN-13: 978-0-8368-9265-9 (lib. bdg.)
ISBN-10: 0-8368-9364-6 — ISBN-13: 978-0-8368-9364-9 (softcover)
1. Wind power—Juvenile literature. I. Title.
TJ820.B46 2009
621.31'2136—dc22 2008012019

This edition first published in 2009 by
**Weekly Reader® Books**
An Imprint of Gareth Stevens Publishing
1 Reader's Digest Road
Pleasantville, NY 10570-7000 USA



Senior Managing Editor: Lisa M. Herrington
Senior Editor: Brian Fitzgerald
Creative Director: Lisa Donovan
Designer: Ken Crossland
Photo Researcher: Diane Laska-Swanke

Image credits: Cover and title page: © Rafa Irusta/Shutterstock; p. 5: © Norbert Schaefer/Corbis; p. 6: © Konstantin Sutyagin/Shutterstock; p. 7: © Eric Gevaert/Shutterstock; p. 9: © Chris Sattlberger/Photo Researchers, Inc.; p. 10: © Tom Uhlman/Alamy; p. 11: © Mike Theiss/Ultimate Chase/Corbis; p. 12: © UpperCut Images/Alamy; p. 13: RobSchuster.com; p. 15: © Chris Howes/Wild Places Photography/Alamy; p. 16: PPM Energy/NREL; p. 17: © Clynt Garnham/Alamy; p. 19: © BL Images Ltd./Alamy; p. 20: Synergy Art: Windside wind turbine in art work Synergia in Oulu, Finland. Design by Pekka Jauhiainen, © Oy Windside Production Ltd.; p. 21: © Paul Glendell/Alamy.



Printed in the United States

1 2 3 4 5 6 7 8 9 10 09 08

# Table of Contents



Words that appear in the glossary are printed in **boldface** type the first time they occur in the text.

# Chapter 1

# What Is Wind Power?

Do you like to fly a kite on a windy day? The air swoops the kite off the ground and tosses it high in the sky. A pinwheel spins in the wind. Wind blows the seeds from a dandelion. The kite, the pinwheel, and the seeds are all moved by wind power.

Wind power makes a kite fly.

Have you ever tried walking into a strong wind? The rush of the air is so strong that you feel as if you will fall down. You have to lean into the wind to keep your balance. You need a lot of **energy** to keep moving forward.

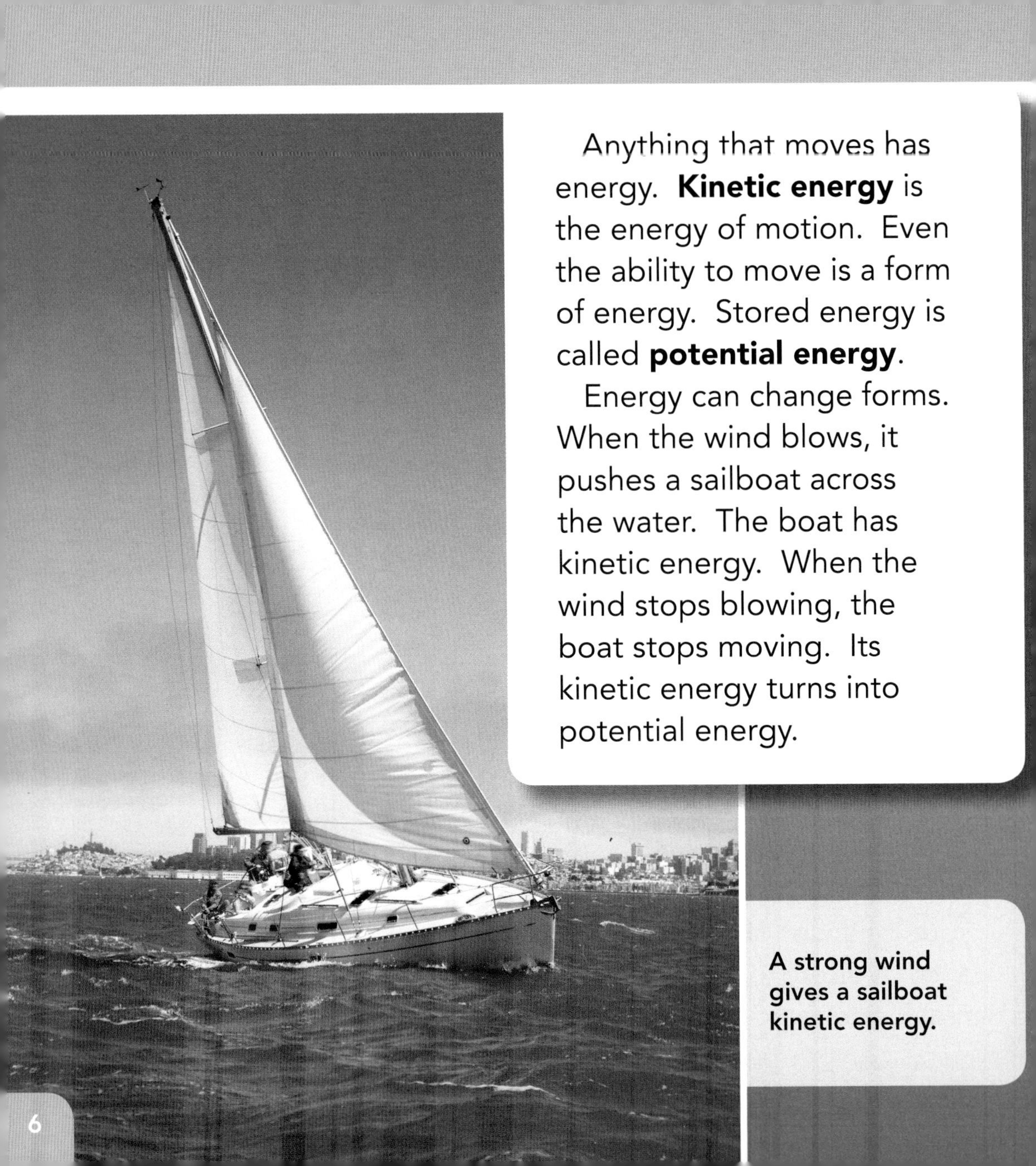

Anything that moves has energy. **Kinetic energy** is the energy of motion. Even the ability to move is a form of energy. Stored energy is called **potential energy**.

Energy can change forms. When the wind blows, it pushes a sailboat across the water. The boat has kinetic energy. When the wind stops blowing, the boat stops moving. Its kinetic energy turns into potential energy.

**A strong wind gives a sailboat kinetic energy.**

Wind power is a source of energy. Getting power from wind is nothing new. People have used wind power for thousands of years. They made sailboats. Later, they built **windmills**. Wind turns the blades on a windmill. Early windmills were used to pump water or grind grain into flour. Today, we can use wind power to make electricity. Electricity powers many things in our homes, such as lights and refrigerators.

A windmill looks like a large fan, but windmills and fans are different from each other. A windmill uses wind to make energy. A fan uses energy to make wind.

## Chapter 2

# Sources of Energy

Wind blows all over the world. Today, however, very little of our energy comes from wind. The world gets about 1 percent of its energy from wind. Where does the rest of our energy come from? Most of it comes from oil, natural gas, and coal. These energy sources are called **fossil fuels**.

Fossil fuels can be hard to find. An oil rig pumps oil from deep underground.

Fossil fuels are made from the remains of plants and animals that lived millions of years ago. People burn fossil fuels to make energy. A power plant, for example, burns coal to make electricity. After fossil fuels are used up, they are gone forever. Fossil fuels are **nonrenewable resources**. They cannot be replaced.

Have you ever seen smoke coming from a factory or from a car? The smoke comes from burning fossil fuels. Burning fossil fuels makes **pollution**. Polluted air is hard to breathe. Pollution in the air mixes with rain and snow that falls to Earth. Polluted water can make people and animals sick.

Cars and trucks burn fossil fuels to drive. Burning fossil fuels pollutes the air.

Burning coal, oil, and natural gas is causing the world to slowly heat up. This worldwide rise in temperature is called **global warming**. Some scientists think that global warming causes more storms. The storms can become stronger, too. Storms with very strong winds, such as hurricanes, can damage buildings and injure people.

**A hurricane is the strongest type of storm. Some of the strongest hurricanes have occurred in recent years.**

Wind spins a pinwheel. You cannot see wind, but you can see things move as it blows against them.

Wind power is a clean source of energy. It does not cause pollution. We will not run out of wind. It is a **renewable resource**. Wind does not stop blowing after it is used for energy. As long as the wind blows, we will be able to use wind power.

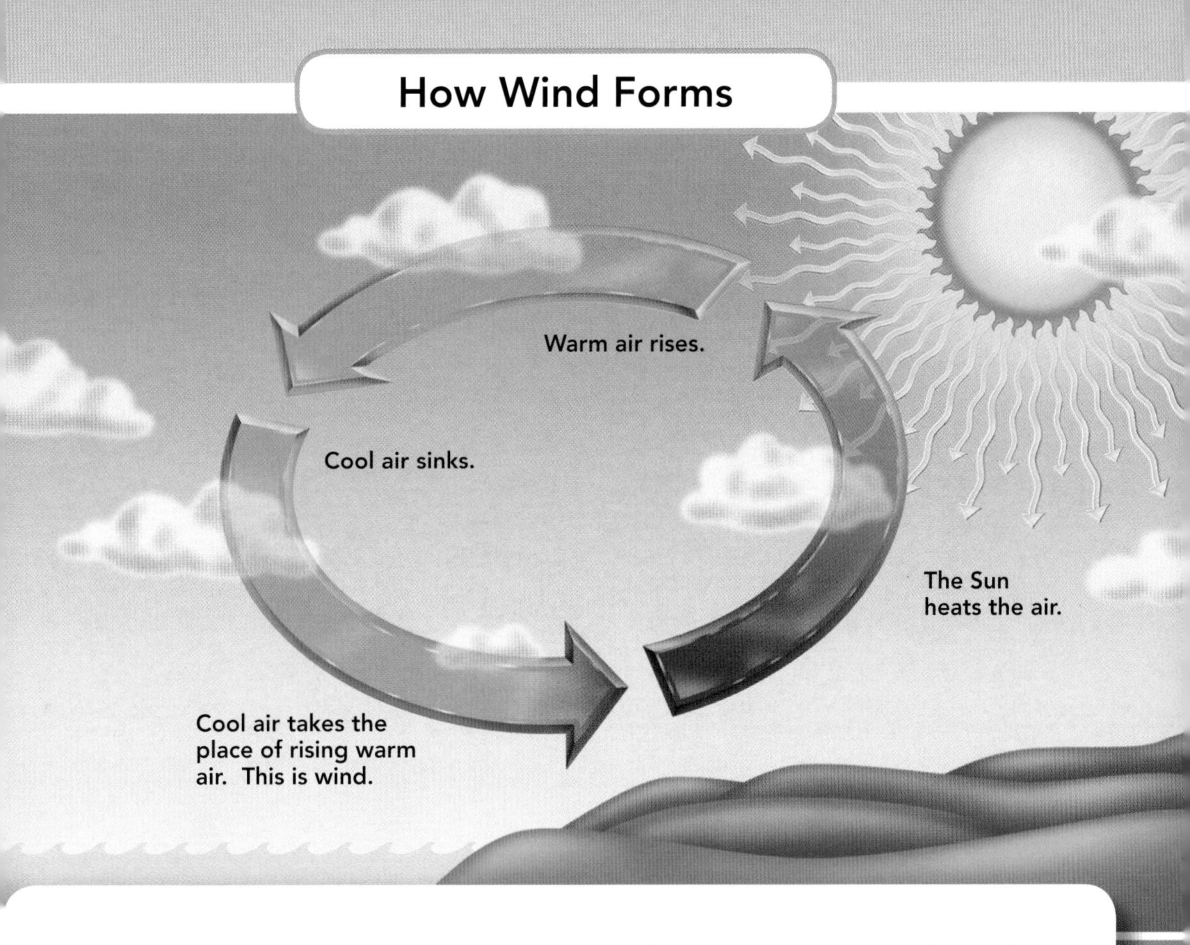


Where does wind come from? Earth's surface is made of land and water. Land takes in the Sun's heat faster than water does. Air above land heats up faster than air above water. Warm air is lighter than cool air. The warm air rises. Cool air moves in to take its place. These changing temperatures make air move and blow in many directions. The moving air is wind.

# Chapter 3

# How Wind Power Works

Today, modern windmills called wind **turbines** make electricity. A turbine looks different from the old type of windmill. Its blades look like airplane propellers. Its tower is usually hollow and made of steel instead of wood. Most turbines have three blades. Many turbines are often built close together to form a wind farm.

Like the old type of windmill, a turbine catches the wind's energy. The spinning blades power a machine called a **generator**. The generator changes wind energy into electricity. The electricity is then sent through cables to a power plant. The power plant sends electricity to houses, schools, and other buildings.

Wind turns the blades of a turbine. A generator changes wind energy into electricity.

Wind blows stronger when it is higher off the ground. The turbines in wind farms are very tall so they can catch more wind. The more wind the turbine catches, the more electricity it can make. Most turbines are as tall as 20-story buildings. Their blades can be 200 feet (61 meters) long. Some turbines are even bigger.

**A truck looks small next to the tower of a wind turbine. These turbines are smaller than most!**

Wind farms work best in areas that have steady, fast winds. Plains and coastal areas do not have a lot of trees or buildings to block the wind. For a turbine to work, the wind must blow from 9 miles per hour (14 kilometers per hour) to 55 miles per hour (89 kph). Turbines will shut off if the wind blows too strong.

**Turbines work best in open space, such as over water. Nothing can block the wind from blowing against these turbines.**

# Chapter 4

# Wind Power in the Future

Today, we get most of our energy from fossil fuels. Wind power, however, is the fastest-growing renewable energy source. At least 39 states have wind power. Texas, California, and Minnesota make the most wind power. The United States plans to get 5 percent of its energy from wind power by 2020.

A good place for a wind farm is on flat, open land, such as a farm or a field.

Some people do not like wind farms. They say turbines are loud and spoil their view. Wind turbines kill birds that fly into the blades. Wind power can also be unreliable. When the wind doesn't blow, turbines cannot make power. Turbines also cost a lot of money to build.

These new wind turbines look very different from other types. They are quieter and safer for birds.

Scientists are working to improve wind turbines. They are making turbines that are quieter and safer for birds. Some new turbines have more sets of blades. These turbines can catch more wind and make more power. Other new types of turbines work even in a gentle breeze.

Some homes get energy from small wind turbines.

Wind will be one important source of energy in the future. Energy from water and the Sun will also help reduce our need for fossil fuels. Using these renewable energy sources will help make our planet a cleaner, greener place to live!

# Glossary

**energy:** the ability to do work

**fossil fuels:** sources of energy, such as oil, gas, and coal, that formed from the remains of plants or animals that lived millions of years ago

**generator:** a machine that makes electricity or other energy

**global warming:** the slow rise in Earth's temperature

**kinetic energy:** energy that is moving

**nonrenewable resource:** a resource that cannot be used again. Once it is used, it is gone forever. Fossil fuels are nonrenewable resources.

**pollution:** harmful materials in the environment

**potential energy:** energy that is stored

**renewable resource:** a resource that can be used again. Renewable resources include air, water, sunlight, wind, and plants and animals.

**turbines:** machines that turn to create electricity

**windmills:** machines that use the power of wind to turn large blades

# To Find Out More

## Books

*Air Pollution.* Science Matters (series). Heather C. Hudak (Weigl Publishers, 2006)

*Generating Wind Power.* Energy Revolution (series). Niki Walker (Crabtree Publishing, 2007)

*Wind Power.* Sources of Energy (series). Diane Gibson (Smart Apple Media, 2004)

## Web Sites

**Alliant Energy Kids**

*www.alliantenergykids.com/stellent2/groups/public/documents/pub/phk_ee_re_001502.hcsp*

Learn more about wind turbines and how they work.

**EIA Energy Kid's Page**

*www.eia.doe.gov/kids/energyfacts/sources/renewable/wind.html*

Read about the ways people have used wind power throughout history.

**Publisher's note to educators and parents:** Our editors have carefully reviewed these web sites to ensure that they are suitable for children. Many web sites change frequently, however, and we cannot guarantee that a site's future contents will continue to meet our high standards of quality and educational value. Be advised that children should be closely supervised whenever they access the Internet.

# Index



## About the Author

Tea Benduhn writes books and edits a magazine. She lives in the beautiful state of Wisconsin with her husband and two cats. The walls of their home are lined with bookshelves filled with books. Tea says, "I read every day. It is more fun than watching television!"